A Dialogue

JAMES BALDWIN NIKKI GIOVANNI

A Dialogue

Foreword by
IDA LEWIS

Afterword by
ORDE COOMBS

J. B. Lippincott Company
Philadelphia • New York

Text copyright © 1973 by James Baldwin and Niktom Ltd.
Foreword © 1973 by Ida Lewis
Afterword © 1973 by Orde Coombs
All rights reserved
First edition
Printed in the United States of America

U.S. Library of Congress Cataloging in Publication Data

Baldwin, James, birth date
    A dialogue.

    Developed from the transcript of a conversation, taped for
the television program "Soul," and first shown in the United States
on WNET-TV, Dec. 1971.
    1. Negroes—Psychology. 2. United States—Race question.
3. Baldwin, James, birth date. 4. Giovanni, Nikki. I. Giovanni,
Nikki, joint author. II. Title.
E185.625.B34   301.45′19′6073   73-4388
ISBN 0-397-00916-X
ISBN 0-397-00948-8 (pbk.)

Foreword
by
IDA LEWIS

Morton, Pennsylvania, my hometown, is a little hamlet tucked beneath Philadelphia. I remember the snows one year when I was seven or eight. I awoke to the silent white world, looking from my window at dawn with the full and wonderful knowledge that I was in love. Later that day at school I could contain it no longer. I wrote him an anonymous note: "Danny, I love you."

Danny, it seemed to me then, was the most beautiful boy in the world; he could accomplish anything. He was Hopalong Cassidy, Gene Autry and Tarzan all wrapped up in one. He was the Shadow, who knew everything despite his mere eight years. He must have known that I loved him. Perhaps he loved me too.

5

How long this love lasted I can't really remember, but once having begun, it seemed to persist forever. I used to do his homework for him. Play football and baseball with the boys . . . just to be in his company. I'd sit in my favorite tree in my backyard and dream of the long exciting trips around the world we would take together. The mountains that Danny climbed in my dreams pierced the highest skies. The wars he fought single-handedly! The awards he won! Danny was the world's darling and most of all he was an ardent defender of my honor.

Years passed by; childhood faded away. Circumstances separated me from my childhood love. I traveled; Danny remained. I went on to higher learning; Danny slipped by the wayside. News about Danny reached my ears from time to time. "Danny got married and beats his wife unmercifully," they said, "and he can't keep a job." "Danny is not the handsome young man you used to know." "You'll be shocked when you see him." "Ida, did you hear Danny is an alcoholic? He turned out to be a no-good man." . . . They said.

"Ida Lewis, is that you?" A familiar voice hardened by a thousand years called out to me. "I'd know you anywhere, anytime. . . . You haven't changed a bit. Don't you recognize me?" He was old, thin and bony. His once-smooth brown skin was weathered by excessive living. His watery eyes blinked teardrops. He tried to stand erect and jerked his head and put out his hand. I reached out; his moist hands clutched mine. He moved his lips to accommodate the cigarette butt that hugged his mouth. I stood still, afraid to change my smile lest I reveal the weak feeling that had overwhelmed me. I wished that

I could thin myself to a shadow. "Of course, Danny, I recognize you. How could I forget?"

"After all these years, it's good to see you," he said. "You look good. I've heard about the great things you've been doing. Always knew as a child that you were somebody special."

"I always thought that you were somebody special too," I said. "I had a crush on you for a long time."

"Yeah," he said. "Things would have turned out differently for me if I had hooked up with you. You could have helped me keep myself together."

"We would have had to keep each other together," I said.

"Keep you together—impossible," he said. "Ladies like you don't need nobody to keep them together. And the black woman . . . she doesn't need anybody."

"Everybody needs somebody, even the black woman," I said like a mediocre philosopher.

I sometimes wonder how the gap between the black man and the black woman grew so vast. We were both on the ships, in the fields, at the whipping posts, struggling in the city. If it's not dignified to push a garment cart, it's certainly not dignified to scrub floor after floor in somebody else's house. America appears to have worked a chemical change on both of us. One piece of litmus absorbing the acid, the other piece throwing it off. Yet both have been tried by fire.

How can the black man view the black woman as anything other than his rib? How long will it take us to realize that pain hurts, loneliness is lonely, fear begets fear? How much further down the road must we go be-

7

fore we begin to draw upon each other's strengths rather than wallow in each other's weaknesses? I think James Baldwin and Nikki Giovanni have begun a significant dialogue in this direction. Two very bright, concerned people communicated to each other their need for each other through the sometimes painful truths which must be shared. To be honest today in this tinsel America one must be willing to put one's soul on the line. Sharing this dialogue will perhaps cause the reader some sad moments. But buildings are demolished to put new buildings up, to start new blocks. Jimmy and Nikki are a cornerstone. The next brick is yours. You can hurl it or you can put it in place. We must learn to keep each other strong; we must renew our commitments to our future. Love, the most vital tool the workman possesses, must not become another relic in our community chest. The journey of a thousand miles, we are told, begins with a single step. I think there is a green valley ahead. We as a people must dedicate ourselves to reaching it. I believe that together we can.

Ida Lewis
New York City
November 1972

Editor's Note

In London, England, on November 4, 1971, James Baldwin and Nikki Giovanni taped a conversation for the television program "Soul!" The program was first shown in the United States on WNET in two installments on December 15 and December 22, 1971. This book, *A Dialogue*, was developed from the transcript of the conversation taped for "Soul!" and includes slight revisions and corrections made in the transcript by Mr. Baldwin and Ms. Giovanni.

A Dialogue

GIOVANNI: Jimmy, I'm really curious. Why did you move to Europe?

BALDWIN: Why or when?

GIOVANNI: Why. I think I know when.

BALDWIN: I moved to Europe in 1948 because I was trying to become a writer and couldn't find in my surroundings, in my country, a certain stamina, a certain corroboration that I needed. For example, no one ever told me that Alexandre Dumas was a mulatto. No

13

one had told me that Pushkin was black. As far as I knew when I was very, very young there'd never been anything . . . As far as my father knew, which is much more important, there'd never been anything . . . called a black writer.

GIOVANNI: I can dig it—those feelings.

BALDWIN: So when I was twenty-four I split and came to Paris and worked and went home in '57. I worked and was based in New York. I was in and out because I was working—trying to write on the one hand, making speeches on the other hand. And I never was able to write in New York, so I would go out and do my work and come back and do my work, if you see what I mean. And then, after Martin Luther King was murdered, I spent a long time in limbo.

At the moment I'm based in the south of France. But there isn't any way ever to leave America. You know, I'd be a fool to think that there was someplace I could go where I wouldn't carry myself with me or that there was some way I could live if I pretended I didn't have the responsibilities which I do have. So I'm a cat trying to make it in the world because I'm condemned to live in the world.

14

GIOVANNI: Condemned?

BALDWIN: Condemned. Condemned. Condemned in the sense that when you're young, and also when you're old, you would rather have around you the expected things, to know where everything is. And it's a little difficult, but it's very valuable to be forced to move from one place to another and deal with another set of situations and to accept that this is going to be—in fact it is—your life. And to use it means that you, in a sense, become neither white nor black. And you learn a great deal about—you're forced to learn a great deal about—the history out of which all these words and conceptions and flags and morals come.

GIOVANNI: There's something that eventually I'm sure we're going to hit. So let's start with "Everybody's Protest Novel," which I think came out in '48?

BALDWIN: It came out in '49, '48, '49—something like that.

GIOVANNI: When I was six.

BALDWIN: Oh, Jesus. \

15

GIOVANNI: I thought it was a magnificent piece. I went to first grade; I said, My God, somebody's really talking. How do you stand in relationship to that now?

BALDWIN: To "Everybody's Protest Novel"?

GIOVANNI: I mean to *Native Son*. Richard Wright.

BALDWIN: What can I say now? Well—

GIOVANNI: What do you think about the younger writers? Within that context are we, in your opinion, moving ahead? Are we moving out of that basic set of—

BALDWIN: It's very difficult for me to say. You know, it can be misunderstood, but you have no idea, and I can never express to you, to what extent I depend on you. I mean you, Nikki Giovanni, and I also mean your generation.

GIOVANNI: My generation?

BALDWIN: Your generation. You have no idea, and I can never express it because in a way I have no right to say it, but I am very proud of you. Something has moved— Things move in a very strange and inexpressible way. If I wrote "Everybody's Protest Novel" today, for example, I would be writing a very different essay out of a very different kind of

16

problem. I think that without quite realizing it and no matter what our hang-ups are as of this very moment—the hang-ups of my generation or the hang-ups of your generation, and the terrible situation in which all of us find ourselves—one thing has changed and that is the attitude that black people have toward themselves. Now within that change—I don't want to be romantic about it—a great deal of confusion and incoherence will go on for a very long time. But that was inevitable. That moment had to come.

In "Everybody's Protest Novel" I was trying—for myself, after all, first of all—to elucidate for myself a theology and the effects of a theology, which I then only realized I carried in myself. You know, it's not the world that was my oppressor, because what the world does to you, if the world does it to you long enough and effectively enough, you begin to do to yourself. You become a collaborator, an accomplice of your own murderers, because you believe the same things they do. They think it's important to be white and you think it's important to be white; they think it's a shame to be black and you think it's a shame to be black. And you have no corroboration around you of any other sense of life. All the corroboration around you is in terms of the white majority standards—so deplorable they frighten you to death. You don't eat watermelon; you get so rigid you can't dance; you can hardly move by the time you're fourteen. You're always scrubbed and shining, a parody of God-knows-what because no white person has ever been as clean as you have been forced to become.

GIOVANNI: Yes, that's true.

BALDWIN: And you know you have somehow to begin to break out of all of that and try to become yourself. It's hard for anybody, but it's very hard if you're born black in a white society. Hard, because you've got to divorce yourself from the standards of that society.

The danger of your generation, if I may say so—you know, we could pursue this at length if you like—is to substitute one romanticism for another. Because these categories—to put it simply but with a certain brutal truth—these categories are commercial categories. There is a reason why, when you and I were slaves, my son, produced out of your body, was by definition a slave. But the master's son—also produced out of your body, depending on his color—if he was light enough he could live in the big house, and if he wasn't he took his condition from the condition of his mother.

18

GIOVANNI: He was still a slave, though.

BALDWIN: He was a slave. He was a slave because even though he might be the master's son, the master could make money off of his son. And the whole institution was threatened if a slave woman could produce a freeman.

GIOVANNI: Of course.

BALDWIN: And the dilemma begins there. Do you see what I mean?

GIOVANNI: And as the dilemma— If the slave—

BALDWIN: The dilemma began—

GIOVANNI: could produce a freeman—

BALDWIN: The slave woman—

GIOVANNI: that means anything produced—

BALDWIN: A slave woman was forbidden by law—I said the reasons were commercial—to produce a freeman, because once you have a freeman out of the body of a slave, you no longer have a slave.

GIOVANNI: That's true.

BALDWIN: And it's very hard to recognize that the standards which have almost killed you are

19

really mercantile standards. They're based on cotton; they're based on oil; they're based on peanuts; they're based on profits.

GIOVANNI: To this day.

BALDWIN: To this hour.

GIOVANNI: Yes.

BALDWIN: Which the church sanctifies.

GIOVANNI: But the church is commercial.

BALDWIN: It's when you begin to realize all of that, which is not easy, that you begin to break out of the culture which has produced you and discover the culture which *really* produced you. Do you see what I mean?

GIOVANNI: Yes.

BALDWIN: What really brought you to where you are. When you're in trouble— When I'm in trouble I do not sing a Doris Day or Tin Pan Alley tune. You find yourself humming and moaning something which—

GIOVANNI: But that has nothing to do with church.

BALDWIN: our grandfathers did. No—

20

GIOVANNI: That has to do with us.

BALDWIN: That has to do with us and what we are. What it's all about is the attempt now to excavate something that has been buried. Something you contain and I contain and which your kid contains and we've got to carry. Something one has to hand down the line for the sake of your kid and for the sake of future generations, and even for the sake of white people, who have not the remotest idea what this means. We have an edge over the people who think of themselves as white. We have never been deluded into knowing, into believing, what they believe. And that sounds like a contradiction. But you watch the man you work for. You have to watch him; you don't know you're watching him.

GIOVANNI: Watching him?

BALDWIN: You're watching him. But he's not watching you. He thinks he knows who you are or what you are. You have got to know who he is because your life is in his hands. And you have to watch him because if you don't watch him you might not live from Monday till Tuesday. It's as simple as that, and without knowing you know him, you know him. He can't fool you. He can never fool you.

21

GIOVANNI: The civil rights movement . . . I came up in the sixties, which is way after everything else. But we always assumed that we knew white people, that we really sort of understood them. And I found out that if you don't understand yourself you don't understand anybody else. And all you know with a snake is to watch a snake. You know it's a snake, but you don't know it—

BALDWIN: That's right, that's right!

GIOVANNI: because there's too much between. There's too much emotion.

BALDWIN: There's too much fear.

GIOVANNI: I can watch the cat I work for, and he's going to watch me to some extent. But we know each other. I would say, I would hypothesize, that he knows me better because his game's running—mine's not. And that's what I've sort of always disagreed about with your generation.

BALDWIN: I see. . . .

GIOVANNI: As long as his game is running, he obviously knows me. He's . . . he's . . . I'm playing, you understand. He says jump, I'm saying how high. He knows me.

BALDWIN: You may be right, but I would put it another way. I would suggest that since his game is running he hasn't got to know you. Because his game is running and you're part of the game he's running, he hasn't got to know you. I would think that one of the reasons Americans are in such trouble now is because the game is running. It was running up until yesterday, really.

GIOVANNI: Would you believe today?

BALDWIN: No. And all of a sudden, to the American astonishment, the American society discovered that other people in the world don't like them. I always knew that because I didn't like them. You know, I love some but—

GIOVANNI: Because they're not likable. There're two people—

BALDWIN: No, they ain't likable.

GIOVANNI: There're two people in the world that are not likable: a master and a slave.

BALDWIN: Exactly. Though we will never, never, never, never get precise categories for that very loaded statement. But that is where the truth is.

GIOVANNI: So the question—I mean, for me—the question has always been power.

BALDWIN: Yes.

GIOVANNI: And for you the question has been morals. I never wanted to be the most moral person in the world.

BALDWIN: I agree, I know what you—

GIOVANNI: I would like— I would sell my soul— You know what I mean? What does it profit a man to gain the world and lose his soul? The world! You know what I mean? The world. That's what it profits him.

BALDWIN: I know.

GIOVANNI: So you take the soul—something that's spiritual. Take the world but give me Jesus.

BALDWIN: Yes, yes.

GIOVANNI: You can have Jesus but give me the world. I'll take it even though it's losing twenty-five percent of its energy every one hundred years or something ridiculous.

BALDWIN: Oh, please don't believe everything you hear.

24

GIOVANNI: No, but it's not my concern. Even though it's polluted, ugly, dirty, give it to me. Or I will take it.

BALDWIN: I agree with you. I agree with you. But speaking for myself and as a representative of my generation— It's probably safer to speak only for myself. In my own case, what I felt and still feel, perhaps in a different way, though I felt it very strongly through the years when we all were marching down those dusty highways with Martin . . .

Look, I left the church when I was seventeen years old and I've not really been to a church since, except when I had to go for various fund-raising rallies or this or that. And I was not exactly the kind of Christian that Martin was, if I could be described as Christian at all.

GIOVANNI: It's hard to be the kind of Christian he was.

BALDWIN: Yes. But I liked him. I loved him, in fact. And I knew that something was happening through him. And my concern was, yes, the world. But I'd seen what white people had done to the world and I'd seen what white people had done to their children. Because in gaining the world they had lost something.

25

GIOVANNI: Their life.

BALDWIN: No. They lost the ability to love their own children.

GIOVANNI: Or the ability to love themselves.

BALDWIN: Which is the same thing. And I didn't want that to happen, if I may say so, to you. It was not a matter of morals so much as a matter of being forced in my case to suggest, to keep suggesting, that though it was indeed a matter of power, power without morality is misleading. Power without some sense of oneself is to me another kind of instability, and black people would then become exactly what white people have become. Do you know what I mean?

GIOVANNI: Yeah, there's a danger.

BALDWIN: I also accept that that danger is— It is not up to me to tell anybody how to run—I can only speak as what I am. I'm a kind of poet and if I'm a kind of poet then I'm responsible, from my own point of view, to the people who produced me and the people who will come after me. So that when the holocaust comes, and it will come eventually—no matter how simple black and white terms may be today, life is not that simple—and sooner

26

or later, if I do my work as I should do it, when I'm needed I'll be there.

GIOVANNI: I think the most important thing I do, the most important thing for any of us, is when what comes or what we know will come comes, we will have the strength to say, Yeah. And I will stay in my apartment on Ninety-fourth and you'll be in Nice. So we'll say, Yeah.

BALDWIN: I will also be able to ride out the storm, but what is more important is not so much riding out the storm for you, Nikki, and me, Jimmy. In my mind's eye there's always that kid. He's going to be here when you're gone. And when I am long gone. So my point of view is that it is about the children. It is about the children. We have to give the children something which in a way was, after all, given to us, though we had to learn how to translate it. Your kid will be moving in a very different world than the one in which I grew up, which he won't know anything about at all. Or the world in which you grew up, which will be remote for him. And yet he comes out of it and has got to carry it much further than you or I will be able to carry it.

GIOVANNI: He's got to have respect for it but not be trapped by it.

BALDWIN: Precisely. You have to both give it to him and liberate him from it.

GIOVANNI: I think that kind of thing has been lacking. I think one of the nicest things that we created as a generation was just the fact that we could say, Hey, I don't like white people.

BALDWIN: It's a great liberation.

GIOVANNI: It was the beginning, of course, of being able to like them.

BALDWIN: Exactly.

GIOVANNI: Which of course upsets them, but that's their problem.

BALDWIN: Yeah, but their problem really is a kind of . . . We were commenting earlier, before this talk began, about the kind of incomprehension in somebody's face when you are trying to describe what to you is a very simple situation.

GIOVANNI: Right.

BALDWIN: People don't like going to jail. You see the man's face; he looks astonished. What? People don't like going to jail? And then you pull back. Does that really go on? You live this all your life. And what you see is that he knows it, really. He doesn't think that you know it. He doesn't think anybody will tell him. And if it comes in, if he allows that to enter into his guts, he's a very different person. He may explode. He doesn't know what will happen if he allows this apprehension of someone else's experience to enter into him.

GIOVANNI: Right, because he's perpetuating his experience.

BALDWIN: And this is the crisis of the age. This is what Malcolm really meant when he said that white is a state of mind.

GIOVANNI: On a certain level, because I tend to be parochial, for one thing, and I tend to care about Afro-Americans, which I would define as the sons and daughters of slaves and slave owners, I have—

BALDWIN: That doesn't, by the way, sound very parochial to me.

GIOVANNI: It's very parochial because I don't care about my third-world brothers and sisters and things like that that I'm sure I should care about.

BALDWIN: You mean you're responsible for a certain situation.

GIOVANNI: I just can't deal with it. I think that if everybody dealt with their own little situation, if I deal with my block and you deal with your block—

BALDWIN: Malcolm said that too.

GIOVANNI: So when we deal with white as being like a state of . . . Well, Malcolm said everything, which I would grant.

BALDWIN: Really?

GIOVANNI: I mean, he encompassed . . . But as we begin to try to deal with the world we find that a lot of things break down. And we find that frequently a white face goes with a white mind. Occasionally a black face goes with a white mind. Very seldom a white face will have a black mind, but we find the frequent situation is that a white face has a white mind. So for the few mistakes that you would make, it's unfortunate. To me it's unfortunate.

BALDWIN: I wouldn't argue with that at all. It doesn't make any difference to me. As I said once, you know that a cop is a cop.

30

GIOVANNI: Well, cops are white.

BALDWIN: Yeah, and he may be a very nice man. But I haven't got the time to figure that out. All I know is, he's got a uniform and a gun and I have to relate to him that way. That's the only way to relate to him because one of us may have to die.

GIOVANNI: You know in New York there's a big campaign going on to humanize the policemen. They have posters, billboards upstate and they have a picture of a big cop bending over this little blond girl—

BALDWIN: Uh huh.

GIOVANNI: and the sign says: "And some people call him pig."

BALDWIN: Uh huh.

GIOVANNI: And I wanted to rent a billboard, I told a friend of mine, and show this big cop and this fourteen-year-old black kid with thirty bullets in him, and say: "And some people call him peacemaker."

BALDWIN: You ought to do it. One thing Lorraine Hansberry said when we had that famous meet-

ing with Bobby Kennedy . . . Lorraine said
to Bobby—who is also dead—

GIOVANNI: Everybody's dead.

BALDWIN: Yeah. Lorraine said to Bobby in answer to
something about black manhood—we had
been talking about black manhood—and Lorraine said she wasn't worried about black
manhood because they've done very well,
all things considered, and she was very
proud of them. But she told Bobby, "I was
very upset about the state of that civilization which produced that photograph of that
white cop in Birmingham standing on that
black woman's neck."

GIOVANNI: What does that say for white manhood?
But, again, that's a moral position, if you
follow what I mean.

BALDWIN: Yeah, I do. I do, I do.

GIOVANNI: That means that we're on top of the situation by being on the bottom. And many of
us—

BALDWIN: I'm not quite that—

GIOVANNI: would like to see it the other way around.

BALDWIN: I'm not quite that romantic or even, if you want to use the word "moral," quite that moral. I simply know— Look, I'm not a financier. I'm not a banker. I'm not a practical man, so to speak. I'm what I am and I know the choices I've had to make in my own life to be able to shave in the morning, look myself in the face in the morning. Now, I'm not so moral as to sit here and say that if somebody had a gun pointed at my brother's head I would pray for him. I'm not about to tell you I'm lighting candles every day and every night for the soul of J. Edgar Hoover. I wonder if I'm moral at all. I don't care at all what happens to Hoover and all his tribe. But I do care what happens to you. And if I am moral, which I don't really think I am, but it's a word that you keep bringing up—

GIOVANNI: I can find another word.

BALDWIN: Yeah, I know. I know, I know. But the relationship of morality and power is a very subtle one. Because ultimately power without morality is no longer power. You cannot call Spain a powerful nation. You can't call Franco a powerful man. He's got a whole nation in jail, but that's not power.

GIOVANNI: No.

BALDWIN: Do you know what I mean?

GIOVANNI: Exactly. His game isn't running.

BALDWIN: Precisely, precisely. Now, when our game starts running—and after all, baby, we have survived the roughest game in the history of the world— You know, we really have. No matter what we say against ourselves, no matter what our limits and hang-ups are, we have come through something. And if we can get this far we can get further. And we got this far by means which no one understands, including you and me. We're only beginning to apprehend it, and you're a poet precisely because you are beginning to apprehend it and put it into a form which will be useful for your kid and his kid and for the world. Because we're not obliged to accept the world's definitions. Just because the white people say they're white, we're not obliged to believe it. Just because the Pope says he's a Christian, we're not obliged to believe it.

GIOVANNI: We'd be crazy if we did.

BALDWIN: We have to make our own definitions and begin to rule the world that way because kids white and black cannot use what they have been given.

GIOVANNI: And they're rejecting it.

BALDWIN: They're rejecting it. Nobody wants to become the president of Pan Am or the governor of California or Spiro T. Agnew. The kids want to live. And we have, out of a terrifying suffering, a certain sense of life, which everybody needs. And that's morality for me. You know, you use the word "morals"; I would use the word "energy."

GIOVANNI: Okay.

BALDWIN: You see what I mean?

GIOVANNI: I can follow that, yes.

BALDWIN: Anyway, it's a very mysterious endeavor, isn't it. And the key is love.

GIOVANNI: It's hard to figure out black people. And that's— No, really, you know . . .

BALDWIN: I know.

GIOVANNI: It's very hard, because you say . . . Let's say somebody— You've been out of the church for a long time, okay? I grew up, of course, in a Baptist church and I really dig the church.

BALDWIN: I do too.

GIOVANNI: I think it's a very cool—

BALDWIN: I do too.

GIOVANNI: I can't dig theology, but the music and the energies of the church.

BALDWIN: Yes.

GIOVANNI: But then I went to the New York Community Choir and heard its anniversary recently—its first anniversary. And then I went up to an A. M. E. Zion church and a lady was singing "Yes, Jesus Loves Me" and people started shouting. People were shouting. And it hit me as I was sitting there—my God, as a so-called black militant I have nothing stronger to offer than Jesus. It blew my mind.

BALDWIN: Baby, what we did with Jesus was not supposed to happen.

GIOVANNI: I believe that.

BALDWIN: We took him. . . . We took that cat over and made him ours. He has nothing whatever to do with that white Jesus in Montgomery, Alabama, in that white church. We

36

did something else with him. We made him
ours. He was always a nigger, we decided,
because Swedes don't come from Israel. You
know, he had to be fairly dark.

GIOVANNI: Well, white people really deal more with
God and black people more with Jesus.

BALDWIN: No, they don't even deal with God. God for
them seems to be a metaphor for purity and
for safety. The whole heart of the Christian
legend has always been in some sense and
sometimes impresses me as being really ob-
scene. And it's the key to all the dirty jokes
which were to come afterwards. Can you
imagine what would happen to you, Nikki.
. . . I'm married to you; I go out to work; I
come home and you say to me, "Baby, you
know what happened today?" I say, "No,
what happened?" "Well, you know, the Holy
Ghost came by." "Oh, he did, did he?" "And,
Joe, you know, the Holy Ghost whispered
in my ear and I'm pregnant." Now I might—

GIOVANNI: I don't think you'd go for it.

BALDWIN: I might, you know, I might look a little hard
at you. If I were really vulnerable I might.
I might try to find that cat, the Holy . . .
the Holy Ghost—the Holy who? And this has
been believed by millions of people who

37

lived and died by it for two thousand years. And when you attack it you're accused of being blasphemous. I think the legend itself is a blasphemy. What is wrong with a man and a woman sleeping together, making love to each other and having a baby like everybody else? Why does the son of God have to be born immaculately? Aren't we all the sons of God? That's the blasphemy.

GIOVANNI: But we're not all the sons of God.

BALDWIN: Well, it depends on what you mean by God.

GIOVANNI: It depends on who's doing it.

BALDWIN: I've claimed him as my father and I'll give him a great time until it's over, because God is our responsibility.

GIOVANNI: Well, I agree with that. A lot of people don't realize that; they think that we are God's responsibility, but there's one of him and what—thirty million of us?

BALDWIN: That's right, and God's only hope is us. If we don't make it, he ain't going to make it either.

GIOVANNI: He'll be in bad shape. People are funny about sex, which I never understood.

BALDWIN: Well, they're terrified, and it's not really about sex. Sex is not really the problem. Love is the problem. When you're a kid— When you're a sixteen-year-old boy or fifteen-year-old boy— You know, a kid doesn't know what he really wants. He wants release.

GIOVANNI: A fifteen-year-old girl—

BALDWIN: There's nothing. There's nothing at that moment that really has to do with love. Love comes much later. For example, a child loves you in a certain way because he needs you. But for men and women it has to be much more reciprocal. You love somebody because you need each other. But one's not capable of this idea when one is a teen-ager—thirteen, fourteen, fifteen—when everything is sexual, when everything is just being discovered. That's why so many of our kids turn into junkies, which we won't go into at the moment.

GIOVANNI: But let's come back to it.

BALDWIN: We'll come back to it. But the great question is not that. The great question, it seems to me, is that the situation of the black male is a microcosm of the situation of the Christian world. The price of being a black man in America—the price the black male has had

39

to pay, is expected to pay, and which he has to outwit—is his sex. You know, a black man is forbidden by definition, since he's black, to assume the roles, burdens, duties and joys of being a man. In the same way that my child produced from your body did not belong to me but to the master and could be sold at any moment. This erodes a man's sexuality, and when you erode a man's sexuality you destroy his ability to love anyone, despite the fact that sex and love are not the same thing. When a man's sexuality is gone, his possibility, his hope, of loving is also gone.

GIOVANNI: He has no way to express—or he has only limited ways to express—love.

BALDWIN: He has absolutely no floor on which to dance, no room in which to move, no way to get from one day to the next. Because to make love to you is not the same thing as taking you. Love is a journey two people have to make with each other.

GIOVANNI: But why do black men, why do we, allow this to happen?

BALDWIN: Look, when one begins to talk about . . . When I begin to talk about the situation of black men with anyone under fifty I've got

40

to avoid sounding in any way defensive. I don't mean that I think you're attacking me. But you asked me a question which I want to answer as honestly as I can, and in order to do so I have to look back over my entire life. You save yourself. If you have any sense at all and if you're lucky enough, you save yourself. You know if you lose your center, and let's say the center is your sex, if you lose that, if you allow that to be destroyed, then everything else is gone. So you have to figure out a way of saving it from the landlord. I mean, I had to watch my father and what my father had to endure to raise nine children on twenty-seven dollars and fifty cents a week—when he was working. Now, when I was a kid I didn't know at all what the man was going through; I didn't know why he was always in a rage; I didn't know why he was impossible to live with. But I had not yet had to go through his working day. And he couldn't quit his twenty-seven-dollars-and-fifty-cents-a-week job *because* he had nine kids to feed. He couldn't say, as our kids can, "I don't like white people." He couldn't say anything. He lived his whole life in silence except in the church. And he couldn't explain—how can you explain to a five-year-old kid?—"My boss called me a nigger and I quit." The kid's belly's empty and you see it and you've got to raise the kid.

41

Your manhood is being slowly destroyed hour by hour, day by day. Your woman's watching it; you're watching her watch it. The love that you have for each other is being destroyed hour by hour and day by day. It's not her fault, it's not your fault, but there it goes because the pressures under which you live are inhuman. My father finally went mad, and when I became a man I understood how that could happen. It wasn't that he didn't love us; he loved his wife and his children, but he couldn't take, day after day, hour after hour, being treated like a nigger on that job and in the streets and on the subways—everywhere he went. And of course when he came home he didn't understand his children at all. They were moving further and further away from him because they were afraid of him, and also, which is even worse, afraid of the situation and the condition which he represented. You know, when you're called a nigger you look at your father because you think your father can rule the world—every kid thinks that—and then you discover that your father cannot do anything about it. So you begin to despise your father and you realize, Oh, that's what a nigger is. But it's not your father's fault and it's not your fault; it's the fault of the people who hold the power because they have deliberately trained your father to be a slave, and they have deliberately calculated that if he is a slave you will be a slave, you will also accept it and it'll go on forever. Slavery will last a thousand years, the slave holder said and believed. And now the bill is in and they want from me or from you sympathy and understanding. I understand it all too well and I have all the sympathy in the world for that spiritual disaster, but I have no pity. The bill is in. We paid it; now it's their turn.

GIOVANNI: It's a funny situation to be in. We were poor but, maybe unfortunately for somebody like me, not poor enough to relate to it. You know, we had enough to eat and things like that. So that my relationship to that whole syndrome, which remains true—I'm twenty-eight—to this day, is that I really don't understand it. I don't understand how a black man can be nothing in the streets and so fearful in his home, how he can be brutalized by some white person somewhere and then come home and treat me or Mother the same way that he was being treated, which perpetuates—

BALDWIN: Yes, of course.

GIOVANNI: I mean, you take somebody like me. I'm not married, right?

43

BALDWIN: Yes, but, Nikki—

GIOVANNI: I—I couldn't play my mother.

BALDWIN: I know, I know.

GIOVANNI: I just couldn't deal with her role. I would say, No, no, no, this won't work.

BALDWIN: But, Nikki, it's also true that since your mother played that role you haven't got to.

GIOVANNI: I couldn't.

BALDWIN: But you haven't got to, that's the point, because she did.

GIOVANNI: But her mother did, you know what I mean?

BALDWIN: Yes, but that's how we got here, and what I'm really trying to say is that I don't want us to underestimate the price paid for us.

GIOVANNI: Oh, I have a great deal of respect for those people, for my parents, for people that I don't know, for everybody who shuffled. But how you could be mistreated and then come home and mistreat someone in the same way is a phenomenon that I do not understand.

BALDWIN: Well, first of all, Nikki, you and I say mistreated, but in the mind of the person who's doing it, he's not mistreating you.

GIOVANNI: I'm not dealing with that. Perhaps in the mind of, let's say, your father or the mind of my father, he is being mistreated. I'm not going to deal with the cracker who is mistreating him. I'm going to deal with him. He knows that he is not being treated with the respect due him as a person, as a black man. In order to get that together, when he comes into the house he begins to brutalize my mother. Which becomes a strange phenomenon to me because I don't like white people and I'm afraid of black men. So what do you do? It's a sad condition.

BALDWIN: Of course it is. This is one of the reasons I try to make clear that the words "white" and "black" don't mean anything. A man comes home; he's in a situation which he cannot control. He is a human being; it's got to come out somewhere. A poor Puerto Rican several years ago, for example—it's a legend, but I can see if this happened why it happened—the cat came home, the three-months-old baby was screaming, as babies do, and he killed it. He didn't mean to kill it, but he picked it up and threw it against the wall.

GIOVANNI: Yeah, but—

BALDWIN: He didn't mean to kill it—it wasn't that. I understand, you know, because I have been there. I know something about that. I don't know what happens to a woman but I understand what happens to a man. You cannot do anything. They've got you; they've got you by the throat and by the balls. And of course it comes out directed to the person closest to you.

GIOVANNI: That's so wrong, because what you perpetuate—

BALDWIN: Nikki, it may be wrong—

GIOVANNI: I hate to use that kind of term.

BALDWIN: It may be wrong, of course it's wrong, but we're dealing with human beings, you know. One cannot be romantic about human nature; one cannot be romantic about one's own nature.

GIOVANNI: Oh, that's not fair. I don't think that I'm romantic for—

BALDWIN: No, I don't mean that you are. But—

GIOVANNI: I have seen how the community . . . And even today, in the seventies, even today there are divisions based on those same kinds of problems, so that black men say, In order for me to be a man, you walk ten paces behind me. Which means nothing. I can walk ten paces behind a dog. It means nothing to me, but if that's what the black man needs, I'll never get far enough behind him for him to be a man. I'll never walk that slowly.

BALDWIN: Nikki, at the risk, at the very great risk of seeming to pull rank—

GIOVANNI: No, pull rank.

BALDWIN: I'm not.

GIOVANNI: Go on.

BALDWIN: No, I don't mean that. What I do mean is that a great many things which seem, if I may say so, new to you are not new to me.

GIOVANNI: Okay.

BALDWIN: So I can say I see what the cat's doing and I can tell you almost exactly how long he will do it. I know, for example, that a great deal of what passes for black militancy right now is nothing but a fashion.

GIOVANNI: At best.

BALDWIN: At best. Of course, something will remain. What is important about it is not the details, not the living people or the living so-called leaders or any of that jazz. What is important is the impulse out of which it has come, the ferment out of which it has come and which it reveals. And what's valuable in it will remain and the rest will go.

GIOVANNI: But what's sort of sad to me is that the same syndrome that our fathers set up—my father is your age . . . well, a little bit older, fifty-five—but the same—

BALDWIN: A little bit older, fifty-five. Thank you, baby.

GIOVANNI: Well, seven years older. But the same syndrome that has been set up and is being perpetuated is that syndrome in which once again the black man is becoming the figure to slide away from. Once again the black man is the figure of whom you say, Well, I can't handle that. And if you visit the States or talk to people enough you'll see that that same syndrome—you know, the little guys that are standing around crossing their arms— They're not lovable, they're not giving any love. They couldn't give a damn about me. And that's unfortunate, because I need love.

BALDWIN: Yes, but, sweetheart, what you're saying is

very, very serious. I'm not in the least deny-
ing it because you're perfectly right. But the
only way we can get through it, I think—
and it's demanding a great deal of you, but
one's got no choice but to demand a great
deal of you—is that you understand. Look,
let us say I'm King Oliver and I'm a pretty
good musician.

GIOVANNI: A very good musician.

BALDWIN: And there's somebody called, let us say, Bing
Crosby, who couldn't carry a tune from here
to here, right?

GIOVANNI: Right. "White Christmas."

BALDWIN: Right? Now I watch this little white boy become a millionaire, become a millionaire
many times over. I can't get a job and time
goes on. You get older, you get more weary,
and since you cannot get a job your morale
begins to be destroyed. Your body begins to
fail, your death approaches—all because
you've never been able to execute what a man
ought to be able to do. And it's not anything
that you have done or not done, but by some
arbitrary sentence. I mean, how in the world,
if I can't get a job, if I can't even get my sax
out of the pawnshop, if I can't even get
money to get on the subway, how am I going

49

to love anybody, except in such an awful pain and rage that nobody could bear it? I'm not trying to defend it; I'm trying to make you see it.

GIOVANNI: I understand what you're saying, but maybe because I'm hopeful or because I've structured my life in a way that I won't—

BALDWIN: I don't, by the way, think that what I'm describing is any longer true for your generation.

GIOVANNI: I see the same syndromes in the same guys that I have to deal with now.

BALDWIN: Yes, but, my dear, my dear, think about the kid. Think about the kid. What you're going through is one thing, and I'm not trying to minimize it—

GIOVANNI: Well, it's not the worst thing in the world.

BALDWIN: The kid is a useful metaphor because it carries you past one moment—

GIOVANNI: Into the next.

BALDWIN: into another moment. No matter what happens to me or to you, one's responsibility is somewhere else. It's a terrible Tuesday and a wretched Friday, but the kid doesn't know that. So you begin to see that what looked so awful on Tuesday or on Friday is awful, but it's not eternal. You can get through it.

GIOVANNI: Hopefully.

BALDWIN: And when you get through it you can understand it.

GIOVANNI: We're not in disagreement. What I'm trying to get you to relate to is that—and I lay it on black men because I'm a black woman—

BALDWIN: You have every right to.

GIOVANNI: I'm sure it's that arbitrary.

BALDWIN: No, you have every right to.

GIOVANNI: Let's say a guy's going with a girl. You're going with Maybelle and Maybelle gets pregnant, and all of a sudden you can't speak to Maybelle because you don't have the money for a crib, right? Maybelle doesn't need a crib. The baby's going to sleep someplace. The baby's going to eat something. But what Maybelle needs at that moment is a man. You see, if the man functions as a man he is not necessarily a provider of all that stuff. In fact, everybody can understand why you can't buy something. You don't have a job; you didn't have a job when you were always going to bed with Maybelle. Why are you going to get a job because she got pregnant? Maybelle understands there is no job. But what she needs is a man to come by and say, Hey baby, you look good. And black men refuse to function like that because they say, I want to bring the crib when I come. You're never going to get the crib.

BALDWIN: Baby, baby, baby—

GIOVANNI: Bring yourself.

BALDWIN: Baby, I agree with you. I agree with you. I understand what you're saying. You may be absolutely right. You are right, from your point of view.

GIOVANNI: It's arbitrary.

BALDWIN: But you have to understand the man's point of view.

GIOVANNI: I'm trying.

BALDWIN: The standards of the civilization into which you are born are first outside of you, and by the time you get to be a man they're inside of you. And this is not susceptible to any kind of judgment; it's a fact. If you're treated a certain way you become a certain kind of person. If certain things are described to you as being real they're real for you whether they're real or not. And in this civilization a man who cannot support his wife and child is not a man. The black man has always been treated as a slave and of course he reacts that way, one way or another. And you can blame him on a human level if you like, but I think it's more interesting to try to understand it, the bag the cat is in. To understand that although I may love you, especially if I love you, in this world I can't come with nothing. It isn't rational. I know it doesn't make any sense, but a man is built like that.

GIOVANNI: Then why talk about the children? I mean, when we talk about my little boy or your nephew, how are we going to create the new child in the same old syndrome? You see, I'm a poor woman. I have nothing; I'll never have anything. I'm looking for beauty in the eyes of those I love or want to love, you know? I'm already deprived of almost everything that we find in the world. Must I also be deprived of you? Somebody has to fake it. Somebody has to say, Hell no, I can't buy you a bicycle. You don't need one. And smile about it so the kid can say, I'm not afraid of Daddy.

53

BALDWIN: Sometimes that happens.

GIOVANNI: But not enough to talk about.

BALDWIN: Perhaps the fact that we're talking about it is important. I've had to learn in my own life that I want something and I want it Friday, and Friday comes and I've worked my behind off to get it and it doesn't come. It doesn't come in twenty years so you use that twenty years. Life is a very short and very long time, and it's very important not to get hung up on any given detail because what is there—like the fact that you're a woman and the fact that I'm a man—that's going to be there forever and we have to deal with that forever.

GIOVANNI: From the beginning.

BALDWIN: And from day to day. But if we love each other we both know it; the tragedy is we both know it, and the greater tragedy is that it's destroyed by things which have nothing to do with you and nothing to do with me. A man is built as he's built, and there's nothing one can do about that. A man is not a woman. And whether he's wrong or right . . . Look, if we're living in the same house and you're my wife or my woman, I have to be reponsible for that house. If I'm not allowed to be responsible for that house, I'm no longer in my own eyes—it doesn't make any difference what you may think of me—in my own eyes I'm not a man.

GIOVANNI: It does indeed make a difference what I think about it, because I could be perfectly willing, and as a matter of fact I *am* perfectly willing, to concede that a man is the natural aggressor. I don't care if I walked up here and said, Let's go to bed; you are the aggressor and that's it, because it all depends on you. I could fool myself. I could fool my friends and say, Yeah, I got him. But it depended on you, you see, so I'm never confused on that level. But I've seen so many people get so hung up in such crappy, superficial kinds of things that, for lack of being able to bring a steak in the house, they won't come. I can get my own damn steak.

BALDWIN: Nikki—

GIOVANNI: I need you.

BALDWIN: But Nikki—

GIOVANNI: And that to me is what the black man has—

BALDWIN: Nikki, you're perfectly right but you're also being perfectly rational.

GIOVANNI: It's a rational situation.

BALDWIN: Yeah, but love is not a rational situation.

GIOVANNI: It must be rational because this irrationality that we have does not work. It destroys people.

BALDWIN: I quite agree with you, but this is something we have to confront. When I was twenty-two I was about to get married and for several reasons I threw my wedding rings in the river and split, decided I would leave. I didn't get married partly because I had no future, and that's very, very important.

GIOVANNI: *You* had no future?

BALDWIN: I had no future.

GIOVANNI: Yeah, okay, whatever you say.

BALDWIN: No, you have to go back to where I was.

GIOVANNI: Yeah, I'm twenty-two.

BALDWIN: I couldn't keep a job because I couldn't stand the people I was working for. Nobody could call me a nigger. So I split to Paris. Now I loved that girl and I wanted children, but I already had eight and they were all starving. And from my point of view it would have been an act of the most criminal irresponsibility to bring another mouth into the world which I could not feed.

GIOVANNI: Yeah, but, you see, those weren't your children, those were your father's children.

BALDWIN: My father was dead, and as far as they knew then—

GIOVANNI: That's not the point. One cannot, and I'm not knocking your life, but one cannot be responsible for what one has not produced.

BALDWIN: I said we are not being rational.

GIOVANNI: But I say we must.

BALDWIN: No, no, no.

GIOVANNI: We must become rational.

BALDWIN: Those are my brothers and sisters.

GIOVANNI: They were your brothers and your sisters, not your children. Anyway, Jimmy, I'd like to know what your feelings are about America. I mean, you live in the south of France, but you retain your U.S. citizenship and you always seem concerned with what's going on in the States.

BALDWIN: Well, as a black man I've paid too much for America to be able to abandon it.

GIOVANNI: I don't think it's a question of abandoning it. I think it's a question of games. If you smile at the white man all day long and come home and abuse me . . . well, it's no wonder he doesn't know you're angry and that the children are afraid. You have to decide who you are going to smile at. Job or no job. Future or no future. 'Cause all those reasons you give me for your actions don't make sense if I can't enjoy you. I think men are very different from women. But I think men build their standards on false rationales. The question is: What makes a man? The question is: Can you be a man wherever you are and whatever the circumstances? We can't abandon America, because where else would we go? I mean, nobody else wants us.

BALDWIN: In any case, my father and my father's father paid too much for it.

GIOVANNI: I've paid too much for it and I'm only twenty-eight. I deserve to do whatever I want to do with it. My son, Thomas, deserves it, whatever that means. I just think that how we go about it and what we're . . . Personally, I'm just not interested in many things that people are interested in. I'm not interested in the President or Congress. I just don't give a damn, because it's just somebody trying to run my life. I'm not interested in movements and ideologies because I think that I would have a difficult time no matter who was in power.

BALDWIN: You'd have a terrible time; I would too.

GIOVANNI: It wouldn't change one bit for me except maybe I would have to go into exile, though of course I could live there.

BALDWIN: That's the tightrope we're on. To come back to the question of white and black, I'm terrified of cultural commissars on either side of the line.

GIOVANNI: The older you get, the more frightening—

BALDWIN: Terrifying, because to be told how to write or what to write about—

GIOVANNI: And it's stupid. The world divides into stupid and intelligent people, weak and strong people, and it's really awful when you can say things like that, but there's so many stupid people.

BALDWIN: The division is not so much between the stupid and the bright. In fact, many of the bright people that I have encountered are wicked. I think the division is between the people who have a certain kind of daring and the people who don't. And the daring is involved with the price you're prepared to pay for your life.

GIOVANNI: Okay.

BALDWIN: You may have been born stupid, but if you're willing to live and take your chances on living, you become very bright.

GIOVANNI: Then in my world that becomes a bright person because it's not based on I.Q.

BALDWIN: Yes, of course.

GIOVANNI: There's a very weak position people get into when they start . . . In the States, I don't know how familiar you are with it, but we're going through a whole thing—there is no such thing as the individual. Which of course is killing the movement.

BALDWIN: That's not true.

GIOVANNI: Oh, it's not only not true, it's stupid. It's killing the movement. And when you see the dumb-dumbs perpetuating that, you don't want to be like them. So the very bright people are saying, Okay, you all can have control, and I hate to watch it because it's destroying what was almost at one point a nation.

BALDWIN: Let it go; don't worry. What you have to do is concentrate on what is essential and not—

GIOVANNI: Essential!

BALDWIN: and not be sidetracked by very disturbing details. After all, you know and I know that the individual does exist.

GIOVANNI: Not only does but should.

BALDWIN: In any case, whether or not he should, he does. I think he should, but in any case he does. And we operate on what we know. We're not obligated to operate out of what Ron Karenga thinks he knows.

GIOVANNI: I'm concerned about it because there are so many young kids who want to believe. When I look at the energy— You know, I teach school, and when I look at my various classes I see those hopeful little faces and I know that they are just as eager to become fascists as anything else. They don't really care what

61

they believe in; what they want is to believe. Then I begin to feel an obligation to say, Okay, try believing in yourself.

BALDWIN: But, my dear, that's all we've been talking about. You call it power, and as you say I do, I call it morals. But it's the same thing; it's exactly the same thing. What one is trying to do is to teach those children something which they will need much later, because they can become fascist very easily, especially if they really believe all the legends which are now being fed to them, such as "black is beautiful." Black is beautiful, and since it's beautiful you haven't got to say so. And it's very important to realize that.

GIOVANNI: The ego is the most important thing about exemplifying that beauty.

BALDWIN: It's a very dangerous slogan. I'm very glad it came along, and it had to come along, but I don't love all black people, you know.

GIOVANNI: True.

BALDWIN: I know deacons, preachers, congressmen, judges, teachers and lawyers who are black, but not like me. And you're trying to tell the child something which transcends all those categories so he won't become what you see all around you every day.

GIOVANNI: One tries. That has to be dealt with because they're constantly being fed, their egos have to be supplemented, in a way which makes no sense to me. Because why should somebody who doesn't even know you run your life? And why should I run some kid's life? I feel eminently equal. I feel like, wow, I would be the person, but why should I do that? Why can't you do it? You can make your own mistakes.

BALDWIN: Yeah, but you have to give the kid the morale which will allow him to do it.

GIOVANNI: But I really see so many games being run by uncreative, stupid people. And it's very disgusting.

BALDWIN: Nikki, most people really accept without very much question the assumptions they're given. When I was growing up, the great trick was getting in civil service and working in the post office. And I can't blame those people.

GIOVANNI: I don't blame them.

BALDWIN: It made them very unattractive people from

63

my point of view, but what else was a black cat to do? You can't create anything unless you have—how you get it I don't know—the belief or the rage or the madness or the necessity out of yourself, or whatever, to do it. Look, read a book by Richard Wright—the late Richard Wright wrote a novel called *Lawd Today*. It's a tremendous book. It takes one day in the life of a black man, a post office worker, and no black cat can read that book and not know it's true. It's a fantastic record. You see, the nature of the drama is that you and I both had to raise the child but I've been destroyed before I get home. You go one way, I go another, and the kid gets lost. And it isn't the fault of the woman or the man, and certainly not the fault of the kid.

GIOVANNI: It's not a question of blame, though, it's a question of responsibility, and it's our responsibility to make sure that kid—

BALDWIN: But what I'm trying to get at, Nikki, is that in order to take the responsibility, you had to be *able* to take the responsibility. It's not a mystical act. Somebody's got to pay the rent, and I can't put you on the streets.

GIOVANNI: The rent has nothing to do with it; that's where we disagree.

BALDWIN: It does for a man.

GIOVANNI: We're back to that. I don't know what it is to be a black man, I will grant you that. But to me the rent has nothing to do with the responsibility that you as a man have to assume with me as a woman.

BALDWIN: If I can't pay the rent I'm not assuming my responsibility.

GIOVANNI: That's what you say. Now what if I say—

BALDWIN: I may—

GIOVANNI: We've tried that! Wait, we've tried that, right?

BALDWIN: Yeah.

GIOVANNI: We have tried to make you able to pay your rent or my rent or our rent. We have found that there are not enough jobs, there's not enough money, for you to do that. Now, why can't we try it my way? And I'm not interested in who pays the rent. I am interested in you.

BALDWIN: Read another story by Richard Wright.

GIOVANNI: Which one?

BALDWIN: A short story called "Man of All Work."

65

GIOVANNI: Yeah, I read it. It's great Wright and it's a great connection.

BALDWIN: So you understand why I have to come back to saying that we're not simply being rational.

GIOVANNI: He castrated himself in a way, if I can say it. He said the only way I can get a job is to be a woman, but he could never be a woman.

BALDWIN: Of course not. But he also said nobody looks at us anyway.

GIOVANNI: Yes, but black men—to me, as a woman, which is all I can say—have to say, Okay, I can't go that route; it doesn't work. And it's so illogical to continue to fight that, to continue to try to be little white men. Which is what you're still trying to be. We have our dashikis and your hair is growing, but you're still trying to be little white men. It doesn't work.

BALDWIN: I agree with you, and I even agree with what you're saying about black women and what you're demanding of black men. I agree with you, but—

GIOVANNI: I demand that you be the man and still not pay the rent. Try it that way.

BALDWIN: All right.

GIOVANNI: Try it, because it's going to be harder.

BALDWIN: All right, all right. But you must understand
            that this is the first time it's been demanded.
            And you must also understand that it can
            be demanded now the way it's being de-
            manded because in fact it's always had to
            happen that way.

GIOVANNI: It has to happen.

BALDWIN: It can be demanded now the way it's being
            demanded only because the objective situa-
            tion, so to speak, has begun to change. My
            manhood is no longer at stake the way it was.
            In a sense we find ourselves in what, to use
            an overloaded word, is a revolutionary situa-
            tion in which one has now to use the women
            and the children. We've been doing that for
            a very long time without knowing it. Now
            we begin to know it.

GIOVANNI: I agree, because I think the only thing that's
            really changed since Martin Luther King,
            since '54, is the black woman.

BALDWIN: No, I don't think she's changed; I think she's
            become more visible.

GIOVANNI: I think she's changed. There was a time when
            my mother and my aunts would say, Okay,

if that's the way you establish your manhood I'm going to go for it. And my generation says, Hey, no good, you must establish a new base. We are, as a group, demanding that a new base be established.

BALDWIN: Yeah, but be careful as a woman what you demand of a man.

GIOVANNI: I demand that he be a man.

BALDWIN: But you can't say you demand it; you have to suggest it.

GIOVANNI: Well, that's your ego that *demands*. No, I demand it. Now, you deal with that.

BALDWIN: All right, okay.

GIOVANNI: In case it was sort of left up in the air or I didn't get it across, I really think that my father, Jones Giovanni, is a groovy cat, and he's lived with my mother for thirty-five years in holy wedlock. I think that's good for them. I think that that sort of thing worked for them. And I think that's the main thing: that they were able to love each other despite everything.

BALDWIN: That's what we were talking about before.

And by the way, you did not have to tell me that you think your father is a groovy cat; I knew that.

GIOVANNI: Yeah, I think he's a gas. I just don't want to marry him.

Let's talk about writing for a moment, because it seems that most black writers at certain points always come back to explaining who they are. They always come back to the personal essay. You've written several novels. One that I happen to love a lot is *Tell Me How Long the Train's Been Gone.*

BALDWIN: I'm glad you like it.

GIOVANNI: I just fell madly in love with it. I gave copies to my friends. I was glad when it finally came out in paperback so I could afford to do what I was doing. But it seems that even though we deal in the novel, deal in fiction, or we deal in poetry, we always have to come back to who are we.

BALDWIN: I don't know. It's an enormous question for me. But there's a moment in *Train,* in the bar in upper New York State, when Leo was watching Jerry, the Italian, and he's watching him as an older Italian who's just come to America is watching Jerry, and Leo thinks to himself that Salvatori understood Jerry

69

because he already existed, in effect, in Salvatori's imagination. And he understood Jerry because of the life that he himself had lived. But no one, thinks Leo, looks at me that way, because I don't exist in anyone's imagination. How can I put it? The reason we are forced to become more and more overt is when you walk down the street—coming back now to the black man/black woman thing—you're my wife and my sister and my mother. I know very well that the people who are looking at you know nothing whatever about you, nothing at all. You know, if it's Marilyn Monroe or Pat Nixon, they know or think they know. But until this century begins to apprehend the experience out of which a Lena Horne comes, for example, or an Ethel Waters or you or Paul Robeson—

GIOVANNI: Or Aretha Franklin.

BALDWIN: Or Aretha Franklin or Ray Charles. White people don't know what they come out of; there's no metaphor in their experience for it —or the metaphor in their own experience is so deeply buried and so frightening. Because, you see, the reason people think it's important to be white is that they think it's important not to be black. They think it's important to be white because white means you are civilized, and being black means you

are not civilized. And there's yet to
hended in any way whatever that
would not be able to walk the street
look at you or you at me, or do
we do in our terrible days, day to day, if we
were not civilized. We represent a civilization. I don't mean merely, literally, the African civilization or the Indian civilization or
whatever. I mean a sense of life, which is the
only thing that civilizes anybody. And which
for mercantile, commercial reasons, to put it
a little bit too simply, the rise of Europe attempted to destroy. I say attempted to destroy because it did not in fact destroy it; it
dispersed it, and under that pressure it began to become something else. What it comes
to is that I am civilized in a way that English-
men are not because I've had to depend on
the principle which Europeans have learned
to distrust. Does that make sense to you?

GIOVANNI: Sort of, on one level, and because I tend to be
slow sometimes, not on another level. What
I'm trying to ask, though, is, do you think you
would ever write a work of fiction or maybe
even a work of nonfiction that did not include
white people? That was just about some
groovy black people that you knew? I mean,
in terms of characters, in terms of who you're
speaking to and why?

BALDWIN: Well, how can I answer it? I'm working on

something now in which there are no white people. But I'm also working on a novel which for the most part takes place in Europe. And, again to put it too simply, it concerns the situation of an Arab in France. Now, in that context I don't know. You know, the Arab is certainly a nigger in France, or he would be a Puerto Rican in New York or a Mexican in California, and what I'm trying to— It's very dangerous to talk about something you haven't finished, but what I'm trying to get at is my apprehension of the crisis of this age. The crisis has something to do with identity, and that has something to do with buried history. Not merely our history that's been buried. When you look at the British, the English working class, that history has been buried too. We were talking about liberation. A writer, whether or not he knows it, always has to go to the source, because there isn't anything else to work from. You can't work from other people's assumptions; you have to work out of what you discover are your own assumptions, and your own assumptions come out of something much deeper than you. And it takes a long time before you realize that there is a connection between *Tell Me How Long the Train's Been Gone* and "Swing Low, Sweet Chariot" or what Ray Charles does with dreary little anthems one wouldn't dream of hearing until he got his hands on them and put our experience into them.

GIOVANNI: Or a ragtime band.

BALDWIN: Yes, and that's what I mean by energy. That, it seems to me, is the assignment of an artist. I am not responsible to anybody but the people who produced me, whether or not they knew they produced me, whether or not they wanted to produce me. I cannot drive a truck and I can't sing a song, but the people who produced me depended on me to do something which they knew before I knew I might be able to do.

GIOVANNI: Yet, and I keep coming back to this kind of thing, there's a whole movement or something that says we have to write only about black people.

BALDWIN: *Tsk, tsk, tsk.*

GIOVANNI: And you have to, you know what I mean? There's a little—

BALDWIN: Look, the very first thing a writer has to face is that he cannot be told what to write. You know, nobody asked me to be a writer; I chose it. Well, since I'm a man I have to assume I chose it; perhaps, in fact, I didn't choose it. But in any case, the one thing you have to do is try to tell the truth. And what everyone overlooks is that in order to do it— when the book comes out it may hurt *you* —but in order for me to do it, it had to hurt *me* first. I can only tell *you* about yourself as much as I can face about myself. And this has happened to everybody who's tried to live. You go through life for a long time thinking, No one has ever suffered the way I've suffered, my God, my God. And then you realize— You read something or you hear something, and you realize that your suffering does not isolate you; your suffering is your bridge. Many people have suffered before you, many pople are suffering around you and always will, and all you can do is bring, hopefully, a little light into that suffering. Enough light so that the person who is suffering can begin to comprehend his suffering and begin to live with it and begin to change it, change the situation. We don't change anything; all we can do is invest people with the morale to change it for themselves.

GIOVANNI: I agree with that. I'm pursuing this because it's something that keeps coming up and I'm personally interested in what you have to say. But the same argument—I agree with you, as a matter of fact—but with the same argument they say, Well, why should a writer be free to write what he wants when a teacher is not free to teach what he wants or a postman—

BALDWIN: A teacher who is not free to teach is not a teacher.

GIOVANNI: That's true.

BALDWIN: If I assume the responsibility, then I have to be free to teach the way I see it. Angela Davis is in trouble not for all those nonsensical reasons given by those impeccable, honorable men, like the governor of California and the head of the FBI, not for any of those reasons, but precisely because she was trying to teach. And to teach in the situation in which black people find themselves, really to teach, is a revolutionary act.

GIOVANNI: You solved it for me! It's something you keep hearing, and they always say, Well, why should the artist be free to do what he wants to do when nobody else is?

BALDWIN: The artist is not free to do what he wants to do; the artist is free to do what he has to do.

GIOVANNI: When, in fact, everyone else should pursue it along those lines. That's wild. I hadn't thought about it that way. That is the God's truth. I've been having revelations a lot lately; it's a personal thing. So what do you think about the trend of black literature from, say, Richard Wright till, let's say, me?

BALDWIN: It's a good—

GIOVANNI: It's a good cutoff point, right here.

BALDWIN: No, it's a good beginning period.

GIOVANNI: Thank you. How do you regard Chester Himes? Chester goes beyond Richard, and since I happen to adore Chester—

BALDWIN: Oh, Chester, yes.

GIOVANNI: Chester's exciting to me because when you go from, say—

BALDWIN: Well, Chester's got guts.

GIOVANNI: My God, *Lonely Crusade*. You're talking about—

BALDWIN: I didn't like *Lonely Crusade* when I was twenty-two.

GIOVANNI: I loved it. I loved it when I read it. I found a first edition—I won't even tell you what I

76

paid for it—and simply adored it. I could see why everybody hated it.

BALDWIN: Let me make a confession. When that book came out I was working for *The New Leader.* I was doing book reviews for ten dollars a shot and going through my own changes, you know. And also—this is very important, really —I was in a kind of political crisis because I had been a kind of communist when I was nineteen.

GIOVANNI: Yeah, whatever one is at nineteen.

BALDWIN: Whatever it means at nineteen. Anyway, I learned a great deal about the American Communist Party, which is an indescribable organization. And since the book in a sense, for me, had the aura of the things I was battling, the political elements I was battling, the book frightened me. In those years—I don't want to get sidetracked with the Communist Party —but in those years the Communist Party was in a sense the only haven for a young American black writer. It was also a terrible trap in which most people lost their lives, because the American Communists were also, after all, Americans, and you worked for them like you worked for everybody else. And since they were Communists you are not supposed to say you worked for them. And all of that complicated my reaction both to Chester and to Richard, in a sense, which it took me a long time to understand. But it's a question of generations again. I had to get to be a man myself, in quite another context. And after the Second World War the American Communist Party was a very different organization, and the black situation became different too, so the Party was no haven at all for black writers. I split. I had to split, otherwise I would be dead. I figured it out in the stones of Paris. Now, Richard left a tremendous testimony about a time that will never be seen again, but which your son will read about the way he reads about Greece. It came out of a set of assumptions which a boy twenty-one—that's what I was then—had to fight if he was going to live at all. What you couldn't accept was that pain; you couldn't accept that past as being your present and, still more, your future. You had to find some way of dealing with it. And to deal with it meant you had to find another vocabulary. You had to risk your life; you had to risk it all; you had to go for broke.

GIOVANNI: Which both Chester and Richard did.

BALDWIN: Now I can see what I owe to Richard and what I owe to Chester, what I owe to Langston Hughes and what I owe to W. E. B.

Du Bois and what I owe to Frederick Douglass. But I could not see that when I was twenty. I don't think anybody can see that at twenty. But you see they were, on one level, simply more exalted victims. A boy named Angelo Herndon, who wrote a book called *Let Me Live*—and I have no idea what happened to him—

GIOVANNI: He's probably dead, like everybody else.

BALDWIN: He's probably dead, like everybody else. And that's your future.

GIOVANNI: Yeah.

BALDWIN: And it takes a long time before you accept what has been given to you from your past. What we call black literature is really summed up for me by the whole career, let's say, of Bessie Smith, Ray Charles, Aretha Franklin, because that's how it's been handed down, since we couldn't read or write, as far as they knew. And it was at one time a crime to be able to read if you were black. It was punishable by law. We had to smuggle information, and we did it through our music and we did it in the church. You were talking before about the church you went to visit. I thought about the Apollo Theater. The last time I saw Aretha, what did she do at the Apollo Theater but turn it into a gospel church service—!

GIOVANNI: Everybody testified.

BALDWIN: And that's true religion. A black writer comes out of that; I don't mean he has to be *limited* to that. But he comes out of that because the standards which come from Greece and Rome, from the Judeo-Christian ethic, are very dubious when you try to apply them to your own life.

GIOVANNI: Dubious?

BALDWIN: I use the word advisedly. So you have to use what, in fact, you have, as distinguished from what you've been told you have.

GIOVANNI: There's a question someplace—I'm trying to form it—and yet I'm stuck with Chester, because among other things he's one of my favorite writers, and I've read everything he's written to date, including his autobiography. But if you move from *If He Hollers Let Him Go* right into *Third Generation, Cast the First Stone*, that group, okay, then he had to stop. Also, he left the States much later than all of you in terms of age.

BALDWIN: Not much ... well, later, in terms of age.

GIOVANNI: He was much older. Then he began *Pinktoes* and went into the Coffin Ed, Gravedigger Jones books, which everybody assumed was safe.

BALDWIN: Everybody?

GIOVANNI: Well, most people. You know what I mean?

BALDWIN: Yeah, I know.

GIOVANNI: They could publish him because they said, Oh, it's just a detective story. Then he did, of course, the master detective story, *Blind Man with a Pistol*, and they said, Who's the murderer? He said, The state's the murderer.

BALDWIN: It's not a detective story at all; it's an allegory.

GIOVANNI: Exactly. And I'm talking about Chester's pursuit of truth. Because Richard Wright died, or was murdered, before he quit pursuing truth.

BALDWIN: That's right.

GIOVANNI: But Chester could say, Okay, I will pursue truth in this way, which looks a little better, so that you can make a movie out of it if you want to and it'll still be true. And then takes it right to *Blind Man with a Pistol.*

BALDWIN: But, sweetheart, it's the same thing we were doing on the plantation when they thought we were singing "Steal Away to Jesus" and I was telling you it's time to split.

GIOVANNI: But why do we—

BALDWIN: Steal away, steal away—

GIOVANNI: Why do we, as black writers, seem to be so hung up on the truth?

BALDWIN: Because the responsibility of a writer is to excavate the experience of the people who produced him. The act of writing is the intention of it; the root of it is liberation. Look, this is why no tyrant in history was able to read but every single one of them burned the books. That is why no one yet really believes there is such a thing as a black writer. A black writer is still a freak, a dancing doll. We don't yet exist in the imagination of this century, and we cannot afford to play games; there's too much at stake.

GIOVANNI: But there has to be a way to do what we do and survive, which is, to me, what seems to be missing.

BALDWIN: Sweetheart, sweetheart, our ancestors taught us how to do that. We have survived until now. You used Chester and it's a very good example. People may think *Blind Man with a Pistol* is a detective story, but he didn't write it for the people who think it's a detective story. There was a very brutal law in America about a thousand years ago which stated that a black man has no rights. This was a law which a white man is bound to respect. I can say now that the people who framed that law have no standards which I am bound to respect. That's the way the wheel goes round. No white critic can judge my work. I'd be a fool if I depended on that judgment.

GIOVANNI: But I'm not sure that *anyone* at this stage—I, personally, hate critics—I'm not sure that anyone—

BALDWIN: Actually, I love critics, but they're very rare. A real critic is very rare.

GIOVANNI: A real critic to criticize a real book would have to write a book of equal length, in which case it's a waste of time because you could read the book they're criticizing. And the young black critics are, I think, just trying to hurt people, and the white critics don't understand. In many cases they would like to praise it but—

BALDWIN: I will be able to accept critical judgments when I understand that they understand Ray Charles.

GIOVANNI: It'll never happen.

BALDWIN: When that day comes, then, okay. That's a new ball game and we'll play it as we see it.

GIOVANNI: I would rather a fourteen-year-old kid said, I didn't like that essay or didn't like that poem. I can relate to that because I know that he read it and that he understood it.

BALDWIN: I held myself together by the judgments of a few people whom I trusted—

GIOVANNI: That's the way it has to be.

BALDWIN: whom I knew would not give me any shit.

GIOVANNI: Beep. It's a funny situation to be in these days because everybody's trying to delineate what you're doing. And to me what's important is that things are being done.

BALDWIN: Look, baby, I know that my mother worked for them for a long time, a long time. She came in their house every morning and left every night, and they did not know anything about her at all. Until they know who their maid is they can't tell me anything about me and still less about you.

GIOVANNI: We were talking earlier about the junkie situation. You say it's related to that whole sexual thing.

BALDWIN: No, no. I was thinking about something a junkie once said to me—a very good friend of mine, a musician. He said, "You're a junkie too." And I thought to myself, Am I? You know, something in the way he said it made me think about it. Because I came from the same streets, I knew why he was a junkie and I knew what had happened to me. He said, "You're a junkie because you talk to yourself." I thought about that, and what he meant was, you have to listen to your own sound; you've got to find a way to listen to your own sound; you live in a kind of echo chamber. And that's true. It also demands a terrible turning away from many things. On one level, some of the junkies I have known have been among the most valuable people I've ever met in my life because they know something—I'm not trying to be mystical about it, but they know their situation. George Cain wrote a novel called *Blueschild*

Baby, which is a tremendous book and the first honest book I've ever read about the condition of a junkie. It really is an exaggerated or, rather, a clear view of the situation of being a black man in America. You can even go further than that and say it's the situation of being a white man, of being a man, in this civilization.

GIOVANNI: That book frustrated the hell out of me.

BALDWIN: It's a tremendous book. Read it again.

GIOVANNI: I will.

BALDWIN: It's a very frightening book. But you have to, in order to live, finally, make so many difficult and dangerous choices that the one thing you're really trying to save is what you lose. And what you're trying to save is your ability to touch another human being or be touched by that person. And when you realize that you can't save that either, you hit the needle. And after all, the junk comes from somewhere. I don't care how many "Cowboys" they throw to the wolves and how many drives against drugs— I lived in the ghetto and I watched it, you know.

GIOVANNI: I think that the biggest hype in the world—

BALDWIN: You buy drugs in the ghetto like you buy whisky in the deep South from the sheriff. It's part of a criminal conspiracy to destroy black people. The proof of this is nobody cared as long as our kids were dying; it's only when the plague spread outward, up to Scarsdale, Westchester, and white kids started dying that we have a drug problem.

GIOVANNI: They have a drug problem. I think it's a big hype, and I'm not on anything, so I don't know it from the inside. But all it's done is to divide the people who are not on drugs, because the junkie and the pusher go on.

BALDWIN: Yeah, the junkie and pusher do go on.

GIOVANNI: They have the love affair. Nobody's going to break them up, but you and I fight about it.

BALDWIN: One of my brothers got robbed by a junkie years ago. He was very hot, very angry; then he realized the junkie didn't have any choice but to rob him. The whole point was to set you at a division. I decided after that the junkie is a victim like me, a brother like me. I ain't no better than he is; I really am not any better than he is. We're in the same trap. We're in the same trap for the same reasons. It's the same way the great powers can use a tribal war in some unknown country. Set them against each other, then blame both parties and put the money in Switzerland, and they—the great powers—still own the country.

GIOVANNI: But both countries are to blame because they should stop and think about it.

BALDWIN: Of course. But, baby, it takes people a very long time to learn very little. If you consider your own life, if I consider my life, when I think how little I've learned in, after all, a fairly long time, and what it has cost me to learn whatever I've learned, and then face whatever it is I've learned, and then act on it, it takes a long time.

GIOVANNI: Sure, but I don't think I'm like that. I don't think I'm exceptional or something like that. But I don't need anything to feel better than I already feel. And I think that junkie hype, that whole war hype, that whole homosexual hype, that whole . . . You know what I mean?

BALDWIN: Do I not?

GIOVANNI: That "he's-not-black hype," I don't need it because it doesn't make me any better.

BALDWIN: People invent categories in order to feel

88

safe. White people invented black people to give white people identity.

GIOVANNI: It's insane.

BALDWIN: Straight cats invent faggots so they can sleep with them without becoming faggots themselves.

GIOVANNI: Somehow.

BALDWIN: Somehow—!

GIOVANNI: But it's a hype.

BALDWIN: If you're a writer you're forced to look behind the word into the meaning of the word.

GIOVANNI: Into the actions produced by the words.

BALDWIN: Yes, you're responsible for what that word means, so you have to find the way to use that word to liberate the energy in that word, so it has a positive effect on the lives of people. There is such a thing as the living word. And that's not a mystical statement.

GIOVANNI: No, it's true. Though I'm just always amazed at the number of hypes people go for. Like if you don't eat meat now you're somehow better than somebody who has a pork chop.

I just can't get over how people continue the B.S. when we see it has nothing to—

BALDWIN: Because they're afraid to let it go.

GIOVANNI: But they're perpetuating their own destruction.

BALDWIN: Tell that to some white South African farmer.

GIOVANNI: I can't tell that to some black guy.

BALDWIN: That you're buying the destruction of your children—

GIOVANNI: He doesn't have to hear it. We talk at cross-purposes sometimes. The white South African does not have to hear me. If his children can't make him listen, how can I? And if I walk down the street and tell some cat, "Listen, so what if you don't eat meat and you eat imported sugar—you're a nigger," he gets mad at me.

BALDWIN: Yeah, but you have to understand why he gets mad at you.

GIOVANNI: Because he is a nigger.

BALDWIN: Right. He's not mad at you; he's mad because you told him the truth. You peeped his hole card. He's mad because he is trying to establish an illusion which you're breaking. He's mad the same way those terrible preachers in the church I grew up in were mad. You know, I began to ask them questions about what this really means. And I began to watch their lives. They were nothing but pimps and hustlers, really. Wrapped in a cloak, in the blood of Jesus and all that jazz. You ask them a real question and they hate you. They hate you.

GIOVANNI: But it's so self-destructive.

BALDWIN: It's got nothing to do with you, and of course it's self-destructive.

GIOVANNI: How are we going to get over that and into—

BALDWIN: Look, baby, I've written off my generation. I don't talk to them. Let's go back to the kid. You talk to those people and he can hear you and you save what you can save. You are not going to live forever either, you know.

GIOVANNI: Thank God.

BALDWIN: What you have to do is make it possible for others to live. That's the only reason to be here. Who needs the rest of it, really?

GIOVANNI: It's so weird, though. It's so counter-productive.

BALDWIN: That's very bad English.

GIOVANNI: Would you say, to sort of sum things up here, that you tend to be optimistic?

BALDWIN: When I pick your kid up in my arms, yes. When I look at you, yes.

GIOVANNI: Not me. I'm very pessimistic.

BALDWIN: Oh no, you're not as pessimistic as you think you are.

GIOVANNI: I'm pretty pessimistic, though.

BALDWIN: No, I think you're pretty realistic. I think you're pretty cool. I think you're pretty clear. But pessimists are silent; pessimists are the people who have no hope for themselves or for others. Pessimists are also people who think the human race is beneath their notice, that they're better than other human beings.

GIOVANNI: People really feel the need to feel better than somebody, don't they?

BALDWIN: I don't know why, but they do. Being in competition with somebody is something I never understood. In my own life, I've been in competition with me.

GIOVANNI: Which is enough.

BALDWIN: Enough? It's overwhelming. Enough?

GIOVANNI: Just by fooling yourself—

BALDWIN: That'll keep you busy, and it's very good for the figure.

GIOVANNI: It makes you happy, you know.

BALDWIN: Well, it means that in any case you can walk into a room and talk to somebody, look them in the eye. And if I love you, I can say it. I've only got one life and I'm going to live my life, you know, in the sight of God and all his children.

GIOVANNI: Maybe it's parochial, narrow-minded, bullheaded, but it takes up so much energy just to keep yourself happy.

BALDWIN: It isn't even a question of keeping yourself happy. It's a question of keeping yourself in some kind of clear relationship, more or less, to the force which feeds you. Some days you're happy, some days you ain't. But somehow we have to deal with that on the simplest

93

level. Bear in mind that this person facing you is a person like you. They're going to go home and do whatever they do just like you. They're as alone as you **are**.

GIOVANNI: Because that becomes a responsibility, doesn't it?

BALDWIN: Well, it's called love, you know.

GIOVANNI: We agree. Love is a tremendous responsibility.

BALDWIN: It's the only one to take, there isn't any other.

GIOVANNI: I agree and it's awful; we're supposed to be arguing.

BALDWIN: And we blew this gig.

GIOVANNI: Goofed again. I think love is an answer but you have to be logical about it, you know.

BALDWIN: You say logical or rational and I say clear, but it becomes the same thing. You can't be romantic about it.

GIOVANNI: No, you can't be romantic about love.

BALDWIN: That's all, you know.

GIOVANNI: I think we're in agreement.

BALDWIN: You think we are?

GIOVANNI: Yeah.

BALDWIN: You asked the loaded question.

GIOVANNI: I asked the loaded question?

BALDWIN: You did. You did ask the loaded question. But it's all right, because we're home free.

IN SEARCH OF A BLACK HEIRLOOM

An Afterword
by
ORDE COOMBS

When I was very young I developed a reputation for being "difficult." No one quite knew what to do with me because the threat of beatings, of starvation and confinement, had absolutely no effect. I simply did what I wanted to do and took my punishment with stoic disregard. My infamy began that June of my eleventh year, when I decided to teach my grandmother a lesson.

She lived near us in a two-story stone house that was almost devoid of furniture, since she had, over the years, given most of it away. Her acts of kindness did not spring from magnanimity but from maliciousness, for if some neighbor failed to do her bidding, she would shout at the top of her lungs and into the tropical stillness:

"Where is my red chair on which you warming your ass? You better bring it back." Not many people took her on and few dared to provoke her.

She was a beautiful woman—part Portuguese, part Carib, with Africa defining the way she walked and the way she held her head—and she never grew tired of telling us how two men went crazy just lusting after her. When I knew her, age had withered her and her breasts had already disappeared. But though she was gnarled and wrinkled, her vanity remained intact, and she constantly asked us: "You like how I looking today?" and our response always had to be: "Yes, Ma, you looking fine."

When she went blind, her rage at the world became limitless, and every day she cursed everyone whose voice she heard. She now spent her days in stormy truculence in the yard of our house, and it was my duty to take her to her home on evenings. Since she could no longer go looking for trouble she turned her venom on her relatives, her grandchildren and my mother, and we had to bear the brunt of her heaping scorn. She loved her son, my father, because he looked like her and because he cherished the sharpness of her tongue. We could not talk back to her, could not retaliate, for we were children and so expected only to be seen and to be spoken to. Childhood for the children of striving middle-class West Indians was something they simply grew out of.

One day Ma was particularly vicious. She accused me of trying to poison her, and when my mother reproved her, she shouted: "Your people was trash, you hear me. Nobody on this island would talk to the likes of you if you didn't bamboozle my boy and get him to marry you."

My mother, who was then so much of a lady that she would not take on an old, blind woman, simply glared at her and went about her business. I went to my father for satisfaction. He laughed. He always did like his mother's acidity, and so he said to me: "You better keep quiet before I put some salt on Ma's tongue and have her put you in your place."

Later that evening I had to take Ma to her house. Usually we followed a direct path, but this time I took her the long way home. I tried to make light conversation, but Ma was silent. She held her left hand to her left ear as if expecting to hear a secret meant only for her ears, and she held the bamboo stick firmly in her right hand. When we got to a gorge (it was not too deep) I simply let go of her hand so that she could fall in. Ma said: "Boy! Boy!" I didn't answer. She opened her legs so that she could balance herself and gropingly felt the land in front of her with her stick. She knew that she was in front of a precipice. She took three deliberate steps backward, then she sat down and began to beat the air in front of her as if to ward off attackers, and her screams caused flambeaux to light up the evening sky and brought the village running to her side.

My father beat me that night until I could not move, and I rewarded his effort with icy silence. The next Sunday I was forced to pray long and hard for my wickedness and then made to sit with my family on the verandah of our home while a tropical downpour washed the streets and water poured over the nearby bridge. Like most parents, mine were determined, as far as they were able, to chart their children's lives, and because they had

99

nothing better to do that afternoon, they asked their three children what we wanted to be when we grew up. I had, by now, made it a matter of policy to speak only when spoken to and even then to be as abrupt as possible, so that when my turn came, I shrugged my shoulders. I noticed, however, out of the corner of my right eye that my father was reaching for his belt. And so in desperation I said: "A bridge, a bridge." Consternation eroded my parents' faces. They didn't think I was being witty, and I had answered them with such obvious sincerity that they couldn't imagine that I was being rude. I was, therefore, odd. I had to be watched over surreptitiously, and any further extraordinary pronouncements would send me to the doctor's office, for I could quite possibly be unbalanced.

I did not know it then but I had acted out of my best interests and I was left alone. I retreated into the world of books and found all the solace, excitement and fantasy a child could hope for. What did my immediate surroundings matter? Why worry about the dust and heat of a Caribbean village; or the Friday noises, when the country people decked out in chambray and satin came down from their thatched mountain huts to appear in court as litigants or to give their meager sums to unscrupulous lawyers? I could not concern myself with the mundane, not when I was fighting side by side with *The Three Musketeers*. I had become a bookworm. My parents did not mind this; in fact, they were quite willing to work hard if their children kept the bargain and brought home good grades. It did not matter what we learned as long as every Friday afternoon our report cards said that we were first in our class in the old gray wooden building known as the Georgetown Government School. My parents did not like my new posture of defiant silence, but every week I reaffirmed their belief in themselves, and they took more than passing comfort in the fact that they had sired intelligent children. Ma was to leave me alone until I grew out of my phase.

It was in September of that year that I first became aware of the possibility of defeat. I had been promoted, and there were several new faces around me when I strolled into the classroom and walked—as was now my right—to the top of the class. I took little interest in the newcomers, partly because I had become a first-class precocious prick who would brook no rivals and partly because the new students were "country bookies," the children of poor peasants who had to walk several miles to school each morning and who arrived with their clothes and bare feet covered with light-brown dust.

At the end of the first week I began to notice Clive. He was, I found out, two years older than I, small, with sharp features and very black. He walked three miles every morning to get to school and had spent the last year trying to support his grandmother. His father and mother were dead, and an ailing uncle had too many children of his own to offer Clive any help. We had no welfare system, and since only the very destitute would crawl to the pauper's asylum, it was every man for himself. I "heard" Clive before I really "saw" him. He was called upon to recite a Wordsworth poem, and his enunciation was so different from that of the other country children that I began to take notice. Obviously I did not pay too much attention, because at the end of the third week my report card said number two. I was furious. I redoubled my efforts and got my parents to hire a tutor. Clive remained number one.

About this time, too, we began to get interested in track, and I was determined to be the best athlete in my school. Morning after morning I would get up at five o'clock and run up the mountains that rimmed our village in order to strengthen my thighs. In the evenings I would train on our playing field until the lights were turned off and crickets and bullfrogs began to claim the tropical night. Then Clive announced that he would enter the competition. He refused to train and looked with such obvious disgust on those who did that my heart strained to beat him so that I could remove the smirk from his face that haunted me as I wrestled with mountain trails in the early-morning dew. I never did beat him, and because I could neither outsmart nor outdistance him, I became his friend.

The next year I was to attend the island's only secondary school that prepared students for college. One of the school's stipulations was that a student had to be under twelve in order to win a government scholarship. Clive had no money and he was overage. No one came forward to help him. He was a country boy who should accustom himself to the smell of cane fields. Clive and I parted. I went to the capital, began to wear khaki suits, sturdy brown English shoes and an orange-and-green cap. I began to walk with the swagger of a member of the St. Vincent Grammar School, began to end my letters with *Per Ardua ad Astra* and learned how to curse.

Clive became an apprentice to a carpenter, and when he was fifteen, left the island to work in the oil fields of Trinidad. I didn't see him again until I was eighteen, full of myself and thinking about attending college. He returned home to bury his grandmother and one rainy afternoon after the funeral we went to a quiet bar. We tried to talk but couldn't. He seemed to have lost every semblance of his former self. He spoke now in clichés, and it was obvious that he had begun to see the world only from the confines of his immediate experience. It was as if society had chastened him and he was beginning to redefine his worth. As I sat beside him I merely wondered how he could allow himself to become so shallow. I did not see that his self-deprecation sprang from his knowing that his best years were being wasted and that he could do nothing about it. And because I did not yet understand that all black people are responsible for each other, I absolved myself from his sliding degradation. Soon the silences between us lengthened. I muttered something about having to study and walked away in the drizzle. I never saw him again, but years later I heard that he had become a policeman and had developed a reputation for brutality.

Last New Year's Eve, thousands of miles away from my tropical island and with the winter face of New York around me, I again began to think about Clive. I wondered what he was doing and how he had come to terms with his faded possibilities. And I thought, too, of the young black men who roam our urban cities bereft of real hope and caught up in the style of spurious priorities. Who will touch them and let them see that

103

their lives belong to them? Their country, afraid of a restless underclass, knows only how to jail them, and poverty programs will not soon end the chaos in their lives.

The New Year's Eve party had seemed deadlier than usual, even though we tried to bring some jollity to the room. We spoke loudly, danced with abandon and promised to give up nothing for the coming year. But whenever the records changed, a stillness descended upon us that gave the lie to our merriment, so that when someone turned on the television and Guy Lombardo appeared, his presence in our living room seemed a fitting commentary on our lack of spontaneity and style.

I couldn't understand why we seemed so listless. It was, after all, the end of a year, and while the wind was screaming down the canyons of our city, we were inside, we had each other and we should have been warm and full of love and hope. But we seemed to be hearing a diversity of rhythms and soon the party broke up, for a clammy lethargy was beginning to envelop us.

Later that morning, when I could see the sun, I tried to put into words the nameless ache that last night had stolen from us our special joys. It was as if with the sixties ended we were pained to welcome another year without any distinctive philosophy—save religion—to guide us as black people. We simply could not define the future. The era of pleas was over. The era of noisy, fervent black demonstrations seemed shrouded in the distant past. The fire had come and black women still saw their sons trapped by the pusher's white magic, their husbands defeated, ultimately, by the scorn in white voices. And while much seemed to have changed, nearly everything remained the same. And so in the center of ourselves we knew that we had to seek new ways if we were to build a spiritual nation on the glacier of North America. It was our uncharted course, our lack of a philosophy, that caused us to wallow in our gloom, for we heard around us discordant sounds and we did not quite know which way to turn.

There were, of course, our artists who would paint our struggles, our poets who would reassure us that the time was ours and our singers who would keen to us the notes of liberation. But we were still too involved in reacting to white patrimony or hostility, and we did not seem to think that we were sufficient unto ourselves.

It can be said, I think, that the artist in our society is no longer the only person who holds up the mirror through which we see ourselves. We are too diverse; we listen to too many gods and dance to too many tunes. The artist, no matter how faithfully he notes his experiences and makes a world from his nucleus, is writing from his bosom and he must hazard certain guesses about people other than himself. A portion of his role, then, as recorder of our woes, our triumphs, has been taken over by the sociologist or the psychologist. It is this man who, with his charts, his red pencils and his tape recorder, hears from a cross section of the populace about the general drift of their lives. It is this man who interprets what the microcosmic sampling says and so projects upon us what we seem to be saying. It does not take much effort to see that *our* sociologists have only begun to focus consistently on what W. E. B. Du Bois started.

It is their task to tell us how we are affected by social stimuli and to bring us out of the shaded melancholia of racial lies.

What, then, will our black sociologists and psychologists be able to tell us about Clive, about his thwarted hopes, his present brutality? And what will they tell us about black men? For until they open our eyes, we flounder, and it will be artists such as Baldwin and Giovanni who, testing the barometer of their own experience, must try to keep us on course, must, in fact, make us see the *life* behind the facts. It is crucial that we understand why we falter and why now we seem to be moving away from the budding spirit of our commonality and back into distrust and glorification of the Head Nigger syndrome. We seem always to be on the brink of a breakthrough, to tether on the edge of that valley where black men—*a priori*—regard each other as brothers, and then to draw back into our faulty beliefs that as Americans we invented individualism and as black people we cannot depend on other blacks when we need them most.

The stories about brothers ripping each other off are legion, and the liturgy of complaints is long. It is not for nothing that a popular Creole proverb states: "What black men do to each other makes God laugh." But when will this sorry charade end? And when will we begin to see that even as my community failed Clive in our feeble response to his ambition, so do black men everywhere continue to fail each other?

At the New Year's Eve party, before we were overcome by stillness, I sat in a corner with an editor and watched several brothers engage in a hearty put-down of each other. They slapped each other's palms; they parried, thrust and then signaled their victory as their opponents were left groping for retaliatory words. It all seemed like good fun to me until my companion pointed out that behind the jokes and the smiles lay a bitter antagonism—a hatred almost—that surfaced when black men, fighting to give some importance to their lives, meet others who are doing the same thing.

"It may be the changes they have to go through that put their priorities off base," she said. "The more I look around, the more I see that our men cannot share themselves. They cannot allow anybody to get too close to them because they don't think much of themselves. So they make a mockery of feelings and they make jiving their special art."

I thought at first that she was overstating her case and told her so, but she asked me why twelve-year-old black boys affected the stances, the grimaces, the inflections of their jiving elders. "It's all a question of style," I said. She agreed, and then said: "These boys in every city have no other carbon to emulate, and so they assume that jiving is their induction to manhood—it is *their* bar mitzvah—and instead of learning that hard work and sacrifice, even in racist America, may bring success, they learn how to profile in front of each other, how to pretend that shadow is substance, and the whole sorry shit goes on from one generation to the next."

I was silent, but it slowly began to be borne upon me that perhaps she was right, and that maybe one dangerous black heirloom that we passed on to our progeny was a healthy respect for falsity. For what, after all, is jiving but refined dishonesty? And how can we call ourselves "natural" men when we have debased emotion to such an extent that our highest accolade is heaped on those cats who, having perfected the art of being cool, now remain impervious to the cries of their fellow blacks? It is natural, it seems to me, to give testimony to one's fears and joys; to make commitment to each other a gem as precious as one's life; and to believe, finally, that our vaunted "image" need not rest on posturing. But we black men carry among ourselves an albatross of mistrust that weighs us down, and it is this and our lack of self-confidence that keep us on our whirligig of unproductive motion. We do not seem to see that no one can cast us into oblivion but ourselves.

I know the lamentations that we raise to excuse ourselves: "Slavery and segregation robbed us of our balls." "Our lack of self-assurance springs from our affinity to failure." "We do not plan for the future because we are convinced that luck is the key to progress and if we are not born with it, our attempts at improvement become meaningless." Much of this is true. Our soaring dreams were always tempered by reality. But we cannot let it go at that, for if luck and fate are our watchwords to progress, then we become impartial witnesses to our own destinies. And if we know some of the reasons for our torment, then self-preservation dictates that we sit down, steady ourselves and avoid the pitfalls.

For while we falter, black women move in the nobility of their purpose and gather strength each day. Again

one hears the explanations: "Black women had to cas-
trate their men in order to keep them alive." "Black
women are the freest people in the United States." But
it seems to me that these clichés, tinged as they are in
defiance, do not explain much. Black women have been
forced to "see" each other and to garner from each
other an emotional strength to face another wearying
day. No matter how bleak her life, a black woman could
cry out from the pit of her soul to another who had already waded through the water and had reached dry
land. She was able to say with candor and emotion:
"That bastard hurt me. He left me unmarried and with
four children and now I will have to fuck with ugly Joe
Young in order to eat. But I still love him." And the
women who heard this lament understood, for like pro-
tagonists in some Greek tragedy, they expected their
lives to be sharpened by pity and terror, but they also
expected to survive. And if the black woman found herself defenseless and wanted by a white man in some
Southern town, she gave him her body but she kept her
soul. She and her friends knew what her options were.
And if, because Sapphires are not supposed to cry, she
held her head high as she walked down Main Street,
how many nights have crept in and heard her singing
her sorrows to responsive ears? Moreover, she knew because she worked in white people's houses that there
was no magic to their material accomplishment. She had
seen her employer relaxed in his home and noted his
archness and his vulnerability. And sometimes she had
listened to the muffled cries of her employer's wife. Be-

cause she had such close contact with the rulers of the world, she could test *their* strength, and when the barriers came down, she already knew *hers*.

It is, I am convinced, a spirit of fellowship, of open and shared pain, that gives our women their fearlessness and makes them the diviners of our future.

At a meeting of poverty workers in New York last fall I sat in agony as the brothers railed against the racism of the Federal government, the state and the city. They repeated statements that we knew to be true, but their sentences gave off heat and no light, and did not tell us how we could proceed with our lives. Money was drying up, they said, because the controllers of the purse did not want black people to prosper. One bearded brother said:

> They tell us to run the programs properly, but they don't want to provide us with decent office space. They don't want to put rugs on the floor, and they think paneling is too good for us.

And as he sat down to cries of "Right on!" a clean-shaven brother said:

> One of the reasons we fail our constituents is precisely because we think that wall-to-wall rugs and paneling are so important. We should concentrate on making sure that our programs are so effective that they become institutions not easily wiped out by the government. We should make sure that our work is of lasting value, and we can only do that if we are prepared to discipline ourselves, to work harder for ourselves than we are used to working for Charley.

There was a momentary silence and then the bearded brother said:

No institutions of importance can remain under our control, because in a racist society nothing we can do will last, and we may as well get all we can while we can.

The crowd shouted "Right on!" again, and this time the clean-shaven brother remained silent. As I left that meeting I felt, suddenly, quite weary, for it was obvious to me that anyone who looks back upon the watershed of the sixties must ask himself what is happening to us. We seem now to be dancing on one infertile spot of weakness, while then we seemed to be on the brink of new discoveries.

It is no longer to our advantage to rant against white people and to continue to see them as faceless blobs blocking our path to self-achievement. Many are racists and, perhaps in perpetuity, many will remain so. Many resent our progress and, far into the murky future, many will continue to try to make our lives a series of concentric hurdles. But our real fight is no longer with them but with ourselves. It is up to us, now that we have pulled ourselves from shame, to set about the awesome task of accustoming ourselves to discipline. We need to gird ourselves with psychological arms that tell us that no victory can be kept by a jiving nation.

If we are to write our future, my generation will have to be a sacrificial one. We will have to sacrifice material rewards and our enlarged egos to see that we lift our young from the slough of mediocrity. It is up to us black

111

men to begin to reiterate to twelve-year-old boys that their lives can be filled with accomplishments if they embrace the rigors of books. I don't really care if most white Americans swim in a sea of mediocrity. I am concerned that black youths drop their posture of "just getting by" and begin to write their names against our widening sky.

There is no reason, except our lack of will, why black boys' clubs should not receive the support of every black man or why, moving away from institutional bureaucracy, we should not use as a living slogan: "Each one support one." For there are many Clives in our world, and only our selflessness and our insistence on performance will save them.

We need, then, to live for each other, for if we do not win our world, the fault will be in ourselves, and we will leave our children foundations no more sturdy than jive and heirlooms no more lasting than yesterday's rhetoric.